ALSO BY STANLEY KUNITZ

Intellectual Things (poems)

Passport to the War (poems)

Selected Poems 1928–1958

Poems of John Keats (editor)

The Testing-Tree (poems)

Poems of Akhmatova (translator, with Max Hayward)

Story under Full Sail, by Andrei Voznesensky (translator)

The Coat without a Seam (poems: limited edition)

The Terrible Threshold (English edition only)

A Kind of Order, A Kind of Folly: Essays & Conversations

Orchard Lamps, by Ivan Drach (editor and co-translator)

The Poems of Stanley Kunitz 1928–1978

The Wellfleet Whale and Companion Poems (chapbook)

Next-to-Last Things: New Poems and Essays

The Essential Blake (editor)

Interviews and Encounters with Stanley Kunitz

Passing Through

THE LATER POEMS
NEW AND SELECTED

Stanley Kunitz

W. W. NORTON & COMPANY

New York / London

The text of this book is composed in Monticello
with the display set in Bodoni Bold Condensed
Composition by PennSet
Manufacturing by Courier Companies, Inc.
Book design by Tree Swenson

Library of Congress Cataloging-in-Publication Data
Kunitz, Stanley, 1905–
Passing through : the later poems, new and selected / Stanley Kunitz.
p.   cm.

I. Title.
PS3521.U7P27   1995
811'.52—dc20   95-2651
ISBN 0-393-03870-X
ISBN 0-393-31615-7 pbk.

W. W. Norton & Company, Inc., 500 Fifth Avenue, New York, N.Y. 10110
W. W. Norton & Company Ltd., 10 Coptic Street, London WC1A 1PU
3 4 5 6 7 8 9 0

CONTENTS

From **THE LAYERS,**
in The Poems of Stanley Kunitz 1928–1978

6

From NEXT–TO–LAST THINGS (1985)

NEW POEMS

PASSING THROUGH

SPEAKING OF POETRY

The writer today, said Albert Camus in his acceptance of the Nobel Prize, "cannot serve those who make history; he must serve those who are subject to it."

How true! And yet one finds to one's dismay that the poetic imagination resists being made the tool of causes, even the noblest of causes. The imagination lives by its contradictions and disdains any form of oppression, including the oppression of the mind by a single idea.

Poetry, I have insisted, is ultimately mythology, the telling of the stories of the soul. This would seem to be an introverted, even solipsistic, enterprise, if it were not that these stories recount the soul's passage through the valley of this life—that is to say, its adventure in time, in history.

If we want to know what it felt like to be alive at any given moment in the long odyssey of the race, it is to poetry we must turn. The moment is dear to us, precisely because it is so fugitive, and it is somewhat of a paradox that poets should spend a lifetime hunting for the magic that will make the moment stay. Art is that chalice into which we pour the wine of transcendence. What is imagination but a reflection of our yearning to belong to eternity as well as to time?

In an age defined by its modes of production, where everybody tends to be a specialist of sorts, the artist ideally is that rarity, a whole person making a whole thing. Poetry, it cannot be denied, requires a mastery of craft, but it is more than a playground for technicians. The craft that I admire most manifests itself not as an aggregate of linguistic or prosodic skills, but as a form of spiritual testimony, the sign of the inviolable self consolidated against the enemies within and without that would corrupt or destroy human pride and dignity. It disturbs me that twentieth century American poets seem largely reconciled to being relegated to the classroom—practically the only habitat in which most of us are conditioned to feel secure. It would be healthier if we could locate ourselves in the thick of life, at every intersection where values and meanings cross, caught in the dangerous traffic between self and universe.

Poets are always ready to talk about the difficulties of their art. I want to say something about its rewards and joys. The poem comes in the form of a blessing—"like rapture breaking on the mind," as I tried to phrase it in my youth. Through the years I have found this gift of poetry to be life-sustaining, life-enhancing, and absolutely unpredictable. Does one live, therefore, for the sake of poetry? No, the reverse is true: poetry is for the sake of the life.

S.K.
1995

from

The Testing-Tree

(1 9 7 1)

JOURNAL FOR MY DAUGHTER

1

Your turn. Grass of confusion.
You say you had a father once:
his name was absence.
He left, but did not let you go.
Part of him, more than a shadow,
beckoned down corridors,
secret, elusive, saturnine,
melting at your touch.
In the crack
of a divided house
grew the resentment-weed.
It has white inconspicuous flowers
Family of anthologists!
Collectors of injuries!

2

I wake to a glittering world,
to the annunciation of the frost.
A popeyed chipmunk scurries past,
the pockets of his cheeks bulging.
As the field mice store seeds,
as the needle-nosed shrew
threading under the woodpile
deposits little heaps of land-snails
for milestones on its runways,
I propose

that we gather our affections.
Lambkin, I care.

3

I was happy you were born,
your banks of digits
equipped for decimals,
and all your clever parts
neatly in place.
Your nation gives me joy,
as it has always given.
If I could have my choice
on the way to exile
I think I'd rather sleep forever
than wake up cold
in a country without women.

4

You cried. You cried.
You wasted and you cried.
Night after night
I walked the floor with you,
croaking the same old
tranquillizing song,
the only tune
I ever learned to carry.
In the rosy tissue

of your brain,
where memory begins,
that theme is surely scored,
waiting till you need
to play it back.
There were three crows
sat on a tree
Sing Billy Magee Magaw.
You do not need to sing to me.
I like the sound of your voice
even when you phone from school
asking for money.

5

There was a big blond uncle-bear,
wounded, smoke-eyed, wild,
who shambled from the west
with his bags full of havoc.
He spoke the bears' grunt-language,
waving his paws
and rocking on his legs.
Both of us were drunk,
slapping each other on the back,
sweaty with genius.
He spouted his nonsense-rhymes,
roaring like a behemoth.
You crawled under the sofa.

6

Goodies are shaken
from the papa-tree:
Be what you are. Give
what is yours to give.
Have style. Dare.
Such a storm of fortune cookies!
Outside your room
stands the white-headed prowler
in his multiple disguises
who reminds you of your likeness.
Wherever you turn,
down whatever street,
in the fugues of appetite,
in the groin of nightmare,
he waits for you,
haggard with his thousand years.
His agents are everywhere,
his heart is at home
in your own generation;
the folded message in his hands
is stiff with dirt and wine-stains,
older than the Dead Sea Scrolls.
Daughter, read:
What do I want of my life?
More! More!

7

Demonstrations in the streets.
I am there not there,
ever uneasy in a crowd.
But you belong,
flaunting your home-made
insubordinate flag.
Why should I be surprised?
We come of a flinty maverick line.
In my father's time, I'm told,
our table was set in turn
for Maxim Gorky, Emma Goldman,
and the atheist Ingersoll.
If your slogan is mis-spelt
Don't tred on me!
still it strikes
parents and politicians down.
Noli me tangere! is what
I used to cry in Latin once.
Oh to be radical, young, desirable, cool!

8

Your first dog was a Pekinese,
fat and saucy Ko-San,
half mandarin, half mini-lion,
who chased milkmen and mailmen
and bit the tires of every passing car

till a U.S. Royal bit him back.
You sobbed for half an hour,
then romped to the burial service
in the lower garden
by the ferny creek.
I helped you pick the stones
to mark his shallow grave.
It was the summer I went away.
One night I carried you outdoors,
in a blitz of fireflies,
to watch your first eclipse.
Your far-off voice,
drugged with milk and sleep,
said it was a leaf
sliding over the light.

9

The night when Coleridge,
heavy-hearted,
bore his crying child outside,
he noted
that those brimming eyes
caught the reflection
of the starry sky,
and each suspended tear
made a sparkling moon.

AN OLD
CRACKED TUNE

My name is Solomon Levi,
the desert is my home,
my mother's breast was thorny,
and father I had none.

The sands whispered, *Be separate*,
the stones taught me, *Be hard*.
I dance, for the joy of surviving,
on the edge of the road.

THE PORTRAIT

My mother never forgave my father
for killing himself,
especially at such an awkward time
and in a public park,
that spring
when I was waiting to be born.
She locked his name
in her deepest cabinet
and would not let him out,
though I could hear him thumping.
When I came down from the attic
with the pastel portrait in my hand
of a long-lipped stranger
with a brave moustache
and deep brown level eyes,
she ripped it into shreds
without a single word
and slapped me hard.
In my sixty-fourth year
I can feel my cheek
still burning.

THE MAGIC CURTAIN

I

At breakfast mother sipped her buttermilk,
    her mind already on her shop,
      unrolling gingham by the yard,
stitching her dresses for the Boston trade.
Behind her, Frieda with the yellow hair,
    capricious keeper of the toast,
      buckled her knees, as if she'd lost
balance and platter, then winked at me, blue-eyed.
Frieda, my first love! who sledded me to sleep
    through snows of the Bavarian woods
      into the bell-song of the girls,
with kinds of kisses mother would not dream;
tales of her wicked stepfather, a dwarf,
    from whom she fled to Bremerhaven
      with scarcely the tatters on her back;
riddles, nonsense, lieder, counting-songs. . . .
      Eins, zwei, drei, vier, fünf, sechs, sieben,
      Wo ist denn mein liebster Herr geblieben?
      Er ist nicht hier, er ist nicht da,
      Er ist fort nach Amerika.
"Be sure," said mother briskly at the door,
    "that you get Sonny off to school
      on time. And see that he combs his hair."
How could she guess what we two had in mind?

Downtown at the Front St. Bi-jo (spelt Bijou)
 we were, as always, the first in line,
 with a hot nickel clutched in hand,
impatient for *The Perils of Pauline*,
my Frieda in her dainty blouse and skirt,
 I in my starched white sailor suit
 and buttoned shoes, prepared to hang
from cliffs, twist on a rack, be tied to rails.
School faded out at every morning reel,
 The Iron Claw held me in thrall,
 Cabiria taught me the Punic Wars,
at bloody Antietam I fought on Griffith's side.
And Keystone Kops came tumbling on the scene
 in outsized uniforms, moustached,
 their thick-browed faces dipped in flour,
to crank tin lizzies that immediately collapsed.
John Bunny held his belly when he laughed,
 ladies politely removed their hats,
 Cyrus of Persia stormed the gates,
upsetting our orgy at Belshazzar's Feast.
Then Charlie shuffled in on bunioned feet.
 We twirled with him an imaginary cane
 and blew our noses for the gallant poor
who bet on a horse, the horse that always loses.
Blanche Sweet, said Frieda, had a pretty name,
 but I came back with Arline Pretty,

and, even sweeter, Louise Lovely.
Send me your picture, Violet Mersereau!
Lights up! Ushers with atomizers ranged
      the aisles, emitting lilac spray.
      We lunched on peanuts and Hershey bars
and moved to the Majestic for the two o'clock show.

                    3
Five . . . four . . . three . . . two . . . one . . .
      The frames are whirling backward, see!
      The operator's lost control.
Your story flickers on your bedroom wall.
Deaths, marriages, betrayals, lies,
      close-ups of tears, forbidden games,
      spill in a montage on a screen,
with chases, pratfalls, custard pies, and sores.
You have become your past, which time replays,
      to your surprise, as comedy.
      That coathanger neatly whisked your coat
right off your back. Soon it will want your skin.

      Five . . four . . three . . two . . one . .
      Where has my dearest gone?
      She is nowhere to be found,
      She dwells in the underground.

Let the script revel in tricks and transformations.
      When the film is broken, let it be spliced

where Frieda vanished one summer night
with somebody's husband, daddy to a brood.
And with her vanished, from the bureau drawer,
    the precious rose-enameled box
    that held those chestnut-colored curls
clipped from my sorrowing head when I was four.
After the war an unsigned picture-card
    from Dresden came, with one word: *Liebe*.
    "I'll never forgive her," mother said,
but as for me, I do and do and do.

AFTER THE LAST DYNASTY

Reading in Li Po
how "the peach blossom follows the water"
I keep thinking of you
because you were so much like
Chairman Mao,
naturally with the sex
transposed
and the figure slighter.
Loving you was a kind
of Chinese guerrilla war.
Thanks to your lightfoot genius
no Eighth Route Army
kept its lines more fluid,
traveled with less baggage,
so nibbled the advantage.
Even with your small bad heart
you made a dance of departures.
In the cold spring rains
when last you failed me
I had nothing left to spend
but a red crayon language
on the character of the enemy
to break appointments,
to fight us not
with his strength
but with his weakness,
to kill us

not with his health
but with his sickness.

Pet, spitfire, blue-eyed pony,
here is a new note
I want to pin on your door,
though I am ten years late
and you are nowhere:
Tell me,
are you still mistress of the valley,
what trophies drift downriver,
why did you keep me waiting?

THE ILLUMINATION

In that hotel my life
rolled in its socket
twisting my strings.
All my mistakes,
from my earliest
bedtimes,
rose against me:
the parent I denied,
the friends I failed,
the hearts I spoiled,
including at least
my own left ventricle—
a history of shame.
"Dante!" I cried
to the apparition
entering from the hall,
laureled and gaunt,
in a cone of light.
"Out of mercy you came
to be my Master
and my guide!"
To which he replied:
"I know neither the time
nor the way
nor the number on the door . . .

but this must be my room,
I was here before."
And he held up in his hand
the key,
which blinded me.

ROBIN REDBREAST

It was the dingiest bird
you ever saw, all the color
washed from him, as if
he had been standing in the rain,
friendless and stiff and cold,
since Eden went wrong.
In the house marked For Sale,
where nobody made a sound,
in the room where I lived
with an empty page, I had heard
the squawking of the jays
under the wild persimmons
tormenting him.
So I scooped him up
after they knocked him down,
in league with that ounce of heart
pounding in my palm,
that dumb beak gaping.
Poor thing! Poor foolish life!
without sense enough to stop
running in desperate circles,
needing my lucky help
to toss him back into his element.
But when I held him high,
fear clutched my hand,
for through the hole in his head,
cut whistle-clean . . .

through the old dried wound
between his eyes
where the hunter's brand
had tunneled out his wits . . .
I caught the cold flash of the blue
unappeasable sky.

RIVER ROAD

That year of the cloud, when my marriage failed,
I slept in a chair, by the flagstone hearth,
fighting my sleep,
and one night saw a Hessian soldier
stand at attention there in full
regalia, till his head broke into flames.
My only other callers were the FBI
sent to investigate me as a Russian spy
by patriotic neighbors on the river road;
and flying squirrels parachuting from the elms
who squeaked in rodent heat between the walls
and upstairs rumbled at their nutty games.
I never dared open the attic door.
Even my nervous Leghorns joined the act,
indulging their taste for chicken from behind.
A glazed look swam into the survivors' eyes;
they caught a sort of dancing-sickness,
a variation of the blind staggers,
that hunched their narrow backs and struck
a stiffened wing akimbo,
as round and round the poultry yard
they flapped and dropped and flapped again.
The county agent shook his head:
not one of them was spared the cyanide.

That year of the cloud, when my marriage failed,
I paced up and down the bottom-fields,

tamping the mud-puddled nurslings in
with a sharp blow of the heel
timed to the chop-chop of the hoe:
red pine and white, larch, balsam fir,
one stride apart, two hundred to the row,
until I heard from Rossiter's woods
the downward spiral of a veery's song
unwinding on the eve of war.

Lord! Lord! who has lived so long?
Count it ten thousand trees ago,
five houses and ten thousand trees,
since the swallows exploded from Bowman Tower
over the place where the hermit sang,
while I held a fantail of squirming roots
that kissed the palm of my dirty hand,
as if in reply to a bird.
The stranger who hammers No Trespass signs
to the staghorn sumac along the road
must think he owns this property.
I park my car below the curve
and climbing over the tumbled stones
where the wild foxgrape perseveres,
I walk into the woods I made,
my dark and resinous, blistered land,
through the deep litter of the years.

SUMMER SOLSTICE

—from Osip Mandelstam

Orioles live in the elms, and in classical verse
the length of the vowels alone determines the measure.
Once and once only a year nature knows quantity
stretched to the limit, as in Homer's meter.

O this is a day that yawns like a caesura:
serene from the start, almost painfully slowed.
Oxen browse in the field, and a golden languor
keeps me from drawing a rich, whole note from my reed.

TRISTIA

—from Osip Mandelstam

I made myself an expert in farewells
by studying laments, the nightfall of a woman's hair.
Oxen chew their cud; anticipation lags;
it is the town's last restless hour;
and I praise that ritual night when the cocks crowed
and eyelids, heavy with the griefs that pass,
opened to the light, while her weeping flowed
into the sound of the Muses singing.

Who knows, when the time comes to say goodbye,
what separation we are meant to bear
and what for us cockcrow shall signify
when the acropolis burns like a flare,
and why, at the new daybreak of a life,
when the ox is ruminating in his stall,
the herald cock, prophetic of rebirth,
should flap his wings on the town wall?

I bless the craft of spinning: the to-and-fro
action of the shuttle, the way the spindle hums.
Look! barefooted Delia, light as a feather,
hurries to meet you, flying as she comes.
Oh, how scrawny is the language of joy,
that weak foundation of our mortal lot!
Everything happened before; it will happen again.
Only the flash of recognition brings delight.

Be it so: a small transparent puppet lies,
like a dried squirrel-skin
extended on a plate,
while a girl crouches, staring, over the image.
Wax is for women what bronze is for men.
We, who move blindly toward a world of shades,
only in battle dare confront our fate;
but their gift is to die while telling fortunes.

THE MOUND BUILDERS

"Macon is the seventh layer of civilization on this spot."
—Ocmulgee National Monument, Georgia

I

Let the old geezers jig on Penn-
sylvania Avenue, and when the jig ends
let them offer a cracked tune
in praise of power:
the State counts the teeth of its friends.
All month, knee-deep in South,
oiled by Methodist money,
I have whirled to a different music
with oversweet, underdeveloped girls
who make me missionary.
My daughter sits in every class;
love is the tongue in my mouth.
Today through the streets of the Greek Revival
and the confederacy of the lawns
trumpeting with azaleas,
my rented Falcon flies
from the tiresome sound of my own voice,
the courteous chicken sitting on my plate,
and Sidney Lanier's exhausted flute
stuck in its cabinet of glass.
What's best in me lives underground,
rooting and digging, itching for wings;
my very worst imaginings
I give to the spoilers of the air.

At the National Park under a sky
of unshattered, unshatterable blue
I rejoice in the prevalence of green
and the starry chickweed of the fields.
Through the millennial ordeal
part, if only part of me, goes down
to the master farmers who built this mound,
this ceremonial earth-lodge,
and locked an eagle in it, shaped of clay,
the fork-eyed spotted bird of their cult,
and piled their dead in mounds higher and higher,
and raised up temple-mounds
to the giver of breath and corn
on which they stacked the harvest fire
that lit this stage for two hundred years.
Fifteen square miles! They must have known their power
stopped by the willows at the river's edge,
and yet it was too much to hold:
only their ghost-song haunts the field.

2

Musician of the lost tribes,
you summon to the council chamber,
to the elders in their scooped-out circle,
an earth-faced chorus of the lost,
people without name to remember,
led by stallion-proud Emperor Brim

bearing his feathered calumet,
chief of the tall Cowetas,
father of the Creek Nation,
by the Spaniards called "Gran Cazique,"
most feared redman of his generation;
foreshadowed, as a scroll unwinds,
by potters out of the swamps
who set their mark on the fanciful pipes they smoked
in the figure of birds or humans,
makers of bowls with carinated shoulders;
and their distant cousins, a patient cloud,
upholding jars with a smooth fold of the lip;
and, more dimly still, the shellfish eaters,
people of the stone axe,
who pitched their noisome camps
on their garbage heaps;
and straggling far behind,
out of primeval murk,
those wandering hunters in search of food
who crossed the land-bridge of the Bering Strait
and sliding over the glacier's edge
paved our first trails with their Mongol bones.
They followed the game that they pursued
into museums of prehistory,
featureless but for the fluted points
dropped from the bloodied mammoth's flanks.

3

The mounds rise up on every side
of a seven-layered world, as I stand
in the middle of the Ocmulgee fields,
by the Central of Georgia Railway track,
with the Creek braves under my feet
and the City of Macon at my back.

THE CUSTOMS
COLLECTOR'S REPORT

For the sake of the record:
      on Tuesday, the 19th instant,
the third day of the storm,
      shortly before nightfall,
they swam over the pass together,
      this pair in their battered armor,
first seen in my spyglass;
      stovepipes assisting each other,
cylinders skating the snowcrust,
      comedians sprawling,
now and then dropping
      under the surface,
perceptible only
      as mounds in the driftage.

To whom, in this trial,
      could I turn for instructions?

At the north wall of the gorge,
      where zero poured to its funnel,
in the absence of guidelines
      I dared the encounter,
half-digging them out
      from the coils of the blizzard,
half-dying of cold
      as I scratched at the ice pack.

Then came issue of smothered voices,
        wind rumbling in empty barrels,
the sound of flags flapping
        in a cave of the mountain;
and the words that I heard
        flew by in tatters:
"nothing . . . nothing to declare . . .
        our wounds speak . . . heroes . . .
unfairly ambushed . . . the odds impossible . . .
        let our countrymen know . . . pride . . .
                honor . . .
how bravely . . . and oh
        what a body-count! . . ."
And the thinner voice cried,
        plaintively winding,
"True, brother, true! but tell me—
        what was the name of our war?"
When I lifted their helmets
        a gas escaped from them,
putrid, as from all battlefields,
        the last breath of the human.
That moment they were lightened.
        It seemed the earth shuddered,
the white tombs opened,
        disgorging their breastplates.
I saw them rise in the wind
        and roll off like ashcans.

Dear sirs, my lords, this
  is a lonely post,
what can I ask but your compassion?
  I petition you for transfer.

THE GLADIATORS

They fought in heavy armor
or, nimbly, with net and trident;
if lucky, against wild beasts,
but mostly against their brothers.

Criminals, captives, slaves,
what did they have to lose?
And the cheers egged them on,
as they waded through shit and blood.

When Claudius gave the sign
the throats of the fallen were cut
in the shade of the royal box:
he fancied their dying looks.

Domitian's coarser itch
was to set cripples on cripples.
No entertainment matched
the sport of their hacking and bleating.

Trajan's phantasmagoric show,
lasting a hundred days,
used up five thousand pairs
of jocks—and the count resumes.

A monk climbs out of the stands,
he is running onto the field,

he is waving his scrawny arms
to interrupt the games.

The mob tears him to bits.
Tomorrow the gates will be closed,
but the promised Crusades will start
with a torchlight children's parade.

THE SYSTEM

That pack of scoundrels
tumbling through the gate
emerges
as the Order of the State.

AROUND PASTOR BONHOEFFER

THE PLOT AGAINST HITLER

Jittery, missing their cues,
Bach's glory jailed in their throats,
they were clustered round the piano
in the Biedermeier parlor,
sisters and brothers
and their brothers by marriage,
rehearsing a cantata
for Papa's seventy-fifth birthday.
Kyrie eleison: Night
like no other night, plotted
and palmed,
omega of terror,
packed like a bullet
in the triggered chamber.
Surely the men had arrived at their stations.
Through the staves of the music
he saw their target strutting,
baring its malignant heart.
Lord, let the phone ring!
Let the phone ring!

NEXT TO LAST THINGS

Slime, in the grains of the State,
like smut in the corn,

from the top infected.
Hatred made law,
wolves bred out of maggots
rolling in blood,
and the seal of the church ravished
to receive the crooked sign.
All the steeples were burning.
In the chapel of his ear
he had heard the midnight bells
jangling: *if you permit
this evil, what is the good
of the good of your life?*
And he forsook the last things,
the dear inviolable mysteries—
Plato's lamp, passed from the hand
of saint to saint—
that he might risk his soul in the streets,
where the things given
are only next to last;
in God's name cheating, pretending,
playing the double agent,
choosing to trade
the prayer for the deed,
and the deed most vile.
I am a liar and a traitor.

THE EXTERMINATION CAMP

Through the half-open door of the hut
the camp doctor saw him kneeling,
with his hands quietly folded.
"I was most deeply moved by the way
this lovable man prayed,
so devout and so certain
that God heard his prayer."
Round-faced, bespectacled, mild,
candid with costly grace,
he walked toward the gallows
and did not falter.
Oh but he knew the Hangman!
Only a few steps more
and he would enter the arcanum
where the Master
would take him by the shoulder,
as He does at each encounter,
and turn him round
to face his brothers in the world.

BOLSHEVIKS

—from Aba Stolzenberg

They came on ponies, barefoot,
brandishing guns that had no bullets;
wore ladies' hats backwards; their leaders
with the look of deacons; and packs
of ox-men, heads wrapped in sacks.

They came in early autumn, shook down
the pears they could not pick by hand;
sprawled across sidewalks and church steps
and felt themselves masters of the land.

The motorcycles spring out of nowhere.
A blast from the roaring White Guards!
Of Trotsky's soldiers nothing remains here
but some sad little mounds near the woods.

THREE FLOORS

Mother was a crack of light
and a gray eye peeping;
I made believe by breathing hard
that I was sleeping.

Sister's doughboy on last leave
had robbed me of her hand;
downstairs at intervals she played
Warum on the baby grand.

Under the roof a wardrobe trunk
whose lock a boy could pick
contained a red Masonic hat
and a walking stick.

Bolt upright in my bed that night
I saw my father flying;
the wind was walking on my neck,
the windowpanes were crying.

THE FLIGHT OF APOLLO

Earth was my home, but even there I was a stranger. This mineral crust. I walk like a swimmer. What titanic bombardments in those old astral wars! I know what I know: I shall never escape from strangeness or complete my journey. Think of me as nostalgic, afraid, exalted. I am your man on the moon, a speck of megalomania, restless for the leap toward island universes pulsing beyond where the constellations set. Infinite space overwhelms the human heart, but in the middle of nowhere life inexorably calls to life. Forward my mail to Mars. What news from the Great Spiral Nebula in Andromeda and the Magellanic Clouds?

2

I was a stranger on earth.
Stepping on the moon, I begin
the gay pilgrimage to new
Jerusalems
in foreign galaxies.
Heat. Cold. Craters of silence.
The Sea of Tranquillity
rolling on the shores of entropy.
And, beyond,
the intelligence of the stars.

KING OF THE RIVER

If the water were clear enough,
if the water were still,
but the water is not clear,
the water is not still,
you would see yourself,
slipped out of your skin,
nosing upstream,
slapping, thrashing,
tumbling
over the rocks
till you paint them
with your belly's blood:
Finned Ego,
yard of muscle that coils,
uncoils.

If the knowledge were given you,
but it is not given,
for the membrane is clouded
with self-deceptions
and the iridescent image swims
through a mirror that flows,
you would surprise yourself
in that other flesh
heavy with milt,
bruised, battering toward the dam
that lips the orgiastic pool.

Come. Bathe in these waters.
Increase and die.

If the power were granted you
to break out of your cells,
but the imagination fails
and the doors of the senses close
on the child within,
you would dare to be changed,
as you are changing now,
into the shape you dread
beyond the merely human.
A dry fire eats you.
Fat drips from your bones.
The flutes of your gills discolor.
You have become a ship for parasites.
The great clock of your life
is slowing down,
and the small clocks run wild.
For this you were born.
You have cried to the wind
and heard the wind's reply:
"I did not choose the way,
the way chose me."
You have tasted the fire on your tongue
till it is swollen black
with a prophetic joy:

"Burn with me!
The only music is time,
the only dance is love."

If the heart were pure enough,
but it is not pure,
you would admit
that nothing compels you
any more, nothing
at all abides,
but nostalgia and desire,
the two-way ladder
between heaven and hell.
On the threshold
of the last mystery,
at the brute absolute hour,
you have looked into the eyes
of your creature self,
which are glazed with madness,
and you say
he is not broken but endures,
limber and firm
in the state of his shining,
forever inheriting his salt kingdom,
from which he is banished
forever.

THE MULCH

A man with a leaf in his head
watches an indefatigable gull
dropping a piss-clam on the rocks
to break it open.
Repeat. Repeat.
He is an inlander
who loves the margins of the sea,
and everywhere he goes he carries
a bag of earth on his back.
Why is he down in the tide marsh?
Why is he gathering salt hay
in bushel baskets crammed to his chin?
"It is a blue and northern air,"
he says, as if the shiftings of the sky
had taught him husbandry.
Birthdays for him are when he wakes
and falls into the news of weather.
"Try! Try!" clicks the beetle in his wrist,
his heart is an educated swamp,
and he is mindful of his garden,
which prepares to die.

INDIAN SUMMER AT LAND'S END

The season stalls, unseasonably fair,
blue-fair, serene, a stack of golden discs,
each disc a day, and the addition slow.
I wish you were here with me to walk the flats,
toward dusk especially when the tide is out
and the bay turns opal, filled with rolling fire
that washes on the mouldering wreck offshore,
our mussel-vineyard, strung with bearded grapes.
Last night I reached for you and shaped you there
lying beside me as we drifted past
the farthest seamarks and the watchdog bells,
and round Long Point throbbing its frosty light,
until we streamed into the open sea.
What did I know of voyaging till now?
Meanwhile I tend my flock, small golden puffs
impertinent as wrens, with snipped-off tails,
who bounce down from the trees. High overhead,
on the trackless roads, skywriting V and yet
another V, the southbound Canada express
hoots of horizons and distances. . . .

CLEOPATRA

—from Anna Akhmatova

She had already kissed Antony's dead lips,
she had already wept on her knees before Caesar . . .
and her servants have betrayed her. Darkness falls.
The trumpets of the Roman eagle scream.

And in comes the last man to be ravished by her beauty—
such a tall gallant!—with a shamefaced whisper:
"You must walk before him, as a slave, in the triumph."
But the slope of her swan's neck is tranquil as ever.

Tomorrow they'll put her children in chains. Nothing
remains except to tease this fellow out of mind
and put the black snake, like a parting act of pity,
on her dark breast with indifferent hand.

DANTE

—from Anna Akhmatova

Even after his death he did not return
to the city that nursed him.
Going away, this man did not look back.
To him I sing this song.
Torches, night, a last embrace,
outside in her streets the mob howling.
He sent her a curse from hell
and in heaven could not forget her.
But never, in a penitent's shirt,
did he walk barefoot with lighted candle
through his beloved Florence,
perfidious, base, and irremediably home.

BORIS PASTERNAK

—from Anna Akhmatova

He who has compared himself to the eye of a horse
peers, looks, sees, identifies,
and instantly like molten diamonds
puddles shine, ice grieves and liquefies.

In lilac mists the backyards drowse,
and depots, logs, leaves, clouds above;
that hooting train, that crunch of watermelon rind,
that timid hand in a perfumed kid glove . . .

All's ringing, roaring, grinding, breakers' crash—
and silence all at once, release;
it means he is tiptoeing over pine needles,
so as not to startle the light sleep of space.

And it means he is counting the grains
in the blasted ears; it means
he has come again to the Daryal Gorge,
accursed and black, from another funeral.

And again Moscow, where the heart's fever burns;
far off the deadly sleighbell chimes;
someone is lost two steps from home
in waist-high snow. The worst of times . . .

For spying Laocoön in a puff of smoke,
for making a song out of graveyard thistles,

for filling the world with a new sound
of verse reverberating in new space,

he has been rewarded by a kind of eternal childhood,
with the generosity and brilliance of the stars;
the whole of the earth was his to inherit,
and his to share with every human spirit.

THE ARTIST

His paintings grew darker every year.
They filled the walls, they filled the room;
eventually they filled his world—
all but the ravishment.
When voices faded, he would rush to hear
the scratched soul of Mozart
endlessly in gyre.
Back and forth, back and forth,
he paced the paint-smeared floor,
diminishing in size each time he turned,
trapped in his monumental void,
raving against his adversaries.
At last he took a knife in his hand
and slashed an exit for himself
between the frames of his tall scenery.
Through the holes of his tattered universe
the first innocence and the light
came pouring in.

THE TESTING-TREE

I

On my way home from school
    up tribal Providence Hill
        past the Academy ballpark
where I could never hope to play
    I scuffed in the drainage ditch
        among the sodden seethe of leaves
hunting for perfect stones
    rolled out of glacial time
        into my pitcher's hand;
then sprinted lickety-
    split on my magic Keds
        from a crouching start,
scarcely touching the ground
    with my flying skin
        as I poured it on
for the prize of the mastery
    over that stretch of road,
        with no one no where to deny
when I flung myself down
    that on the given course
        I was the world's fastest human.

2

Around the bend
    that tried to loop me home
        dawdling came natural

across a nettled field
    riddled with rabbit-life
        where the bees sank sugar-wells
in the trunks of the maples
    and a stringy old lilac
        more than two stories tall
blazing with mildew
    remembered a door in the
        long teeth of the woods.
All of it happened slow:
    brushing the stickseed off,
        wading through jewelweed
strangled by angel's hair,
    spotting the print of the deer
        and the red fox's scats.

Once I owned the key
    to an umbrageous trail
        thickened with mosses
where flickering presences
    gave me right of passage
        as I followed in the steps
of straight-backed Massassoit
    soundlessly heel-and-toe
        practicing my Indian walk.

3

Past the abandoned quarry
    where the pale sun bobbed
        in the sump of the granite,
past copperhead ledge,
    where the ferns gave foothold,
        I walked, deliberate,
on to the clearing,
    with the stones in my pocket
        changing to oracles
and my coiled ear tuned
    to the slightest leaf-stir.
        I had kept my appointment.
There I stood in the shadow,
    at fifty measured paces,
        of the inexhaustible oak,
tyrant and target,
    Jehovah of acorns,
        watchtower of the thunders,
that locked King Philip's War
    in its annulated core
        under the cut of my name.
Father wherever you are
    I have only three throws
        bless my good right arm.
In the haze of afternoon,
    while the air flowed saffron,
        I played my game for keeps—

for love, for poetry,
    and for eternal life—
        after the trials of summer.

4

In the recurring dream
    my mother stands
        in her bridal gown
under the burning lilac,
    with Bernard Shaw and Bertie
        Russell kissing her hands;
the house behind her is in ruins;
    she is wearing an owl's face
        and makes barking noises.
Her minatory finger points.
    I pass through the cardboard doorway
        askew in the field
and peer down a well
    where an albino walrus huffs.
        He has the gentlest eyes.
If the dirt keeps sifting in,
    staining the water yellow,
        why should I be blamed?
Never try to explain.
    That single Model A
        sputtering up the grade

unfurled a highway behind
        where the tanks maneuver,
            revolving their turrets.
In a murderous time
        the heart breaks and breaks
            and lives by breaking.
It is necessary to go
        through dark and deeper dark
            and not to turn.
I am looking for the trail.
        Where is my testing-tree?
            Give me back my stones!

THE GAME

Let's spin the bottle
No I don't want to be kissed

Sometimes I feel my arm
Is turning into a tree

Or hardening to stone
Past memory of green

I've a long way to go
Who never learned to pray

O the night is coming on
And I am nobody's son

Father it's true
But only for a day.

The Layers

from

The Poems of Stanley Kunitz 1928–1978

THE KNOT

I've tried to seal it in,
that cross-grained knot
on the opposite wall,
scored in the lintel of my door,
but it keeps bleeding through
into the world we share.
Mornings when I wake,
curled in my web,
I hear it come
with a rush of resin
out of the trauma
of its lopping-off.
Obstinate bud,
sticky with life,
mad for the rain again,
it racks itself with shoots
that crackle overhead,
dividing as they grow.
Let be! Let be!
I shake my wings
and fly into its boughs.

WHAT OF THE NIGHT?

I

One summer, like a stone
dropped down a well,
I sank into myself
and raked
the bottom slime.
When I stretched out my thigh
it touched the dark,
and the dark rolled over me.
A brackish life
filled the cups of my skin.
Then gradually I heard
above the steady
breathing of the land
a high, inhuman chord
light-years away,
out of a cleaner space,
a more innocent age,
as when pilot angels
with crystal eyes and streaming hair
rode planets through the skies,
and each one sang
a single ravishing note
that melted
into the music of the spheres.

2

What wakes me now
like the country doctor
startled in his sleep?
Why does my racing heart
shuffle down the hall
for the hundredth time
to answer the night-bell?
Whoever summons me has need of me.
How could I afford
to disobey that call?
A gentle, insistent ring
pulled me from my bed,
from loving arms,
though I know
I am not ready yet
and nobody stands on the stoop,
not even a stray cat
slouches under the sodium lamp.
Deceived! or self-deceived.
I can never atone for it.
Oh I should be the one
to swell the night with my alarm!
When the messenger comes again
I shall pretend
in a childish voice
my father is not home.

QUINNAPOXET

I was fishing in the abandoned reservoir
back in Quinnapoxet,
where the snapping turtles cruised
and the bullheads swayed
in their bower of tree-stumps,
sleek as eels and pigeon-fat.
One of them gashed my thumb
with a flick of his razor fin
when I yanked the barb
out of his gullet.
The sun hung its terrible coals
over Buteau's farm: I saw
the treetops seething.

They came suddenly into view
on the Indian road,
evenly stepping
past the apple orchard,
commingling with the dust
they raised, their cloud of being,
against the dripping light
looming larger and bolder.
She was wearing a mourning bonnet
and a wrap of shining taffeta.
"Why don't you write?" she cried
from the folds of her veil.
"We never hear from you."

I had nothing to say to her.
But for him who walked behind her
in his dark worsted suit,
with his face averted
as if to hide a scald,
deep in his other life,
I touched my forehead
with my swollen thumb
and splayed my fingers out—
in deaf-mute country
the sign for father.

WORDS FOR THE
UNKNOWN MAKERS

A Garland of Commemorative Verses*

TO A SLAVE NAMED JOB

Dreaming of Africa
and the kings of the dark land,
bearer of a suffering name,
you carved this Indian
out of a man-sized log
to be your surrogate
and avatar.
Outside the smoke-shop
he stands aloof and bold,
with his raised foot poised
for the oppressor's neck.
The cigars he offers
are not for sale.
They fit his hand
as though they were a gun.

---

* On the occasion of the exhibition "The Flowering of American Folk Art," at the Whitney Museum in 1974. See Note on p. 165.

SACRED TO THE MEMORY

Mourn for Polly Botsford, aged thirty-nine,
and for her blossom Polly, one year old,
and for Gideon, her infant son, nipped in the bud.
And mourn for the mourners under the graveside willow,
trailing its branches of inverted V's,
those women propped like bookends on either side of the
    tomb,
and that brace of innocents in matching calico
linked to their mother's grief with a zigzag clasp of hands,
as proper in their place as stepping-stones.
Mourn, too, for the nameless painter of the scene
who, like them all, was born to walk a while
beside the brook whose source is common tears,
till suddenly it's time to unlatch the narrow gate
and pass through the church that is not made with walls
and seek another home, a different sky.

GIRL WITH SAMPLER

"A Soft Answer Turneth Away Wrath"

She sat by the window,
lips pursed, plying her needle.
The parlor wall waited
for a family showpiece.
"Do it right, child!" said her mother.
This way she learned the ABC's,
improved her mind with Bible verses,
embroidered her name into her dowry:
Nabby Dexter of Providence, Rhode Island,
Patricia Goodeshall, Abigail Fleetwood,
Elizabeth Finney, virtuoso of stitches
(cross . . . flat . . . buttonhole . . .
satin . . . outline . . . bullion knot).
Some prized the task and its performance,
others groaned as they ripped out blunders
in and around the moral sentences.
One of them added a line to her sampler:
"And Hated every bit of it."

TROMPE L'OEIL

Whoever made this piece began
with boards of honest country pine
fit for a modest sideboard table.
As for finishing,
I doubt he had a plan,
he simply led his brushes on,
or maybe it was they that led,
stippling and graining,
simulating to a T
maple, walnut, birch,
imitating inlays and veneers,
putting on the airs of Sheraton.
Utility took fantasy for wife.
O lucky day!
The fun was in the afterplay
when the true artisan
tells his white lies.

A BLESSING OF WOMEN

"Remember me is all I ask,
And, if remembered be a task,
Forget me."
>—Album verses by Minerva Butler Miller,
>tinsmith's daughter, peddler's wife, c. 1850

BLESS ZERUAH HIGLEY GUERNSEY of Castleton, Vermont, who sheared the wool from her father's sheep; washed, carded, and spun it into yarn; steeped it in dyes concocted from native berries, barks, and plants; and embroidered it, in Double Kensington chain stitch, on a ground of homespun squares until they bloomed with fruit, shells, snow crystals, flowers, and cats, most singularly a noble blue cat; each of the eighty-odd panels being different from the rest, and the whole a paragon of American needlework design, executed in the ardor of her long pre-nuptial flight, and accomplished in 1835 for her ill-starred wedding day.

BLESS DEBORAH GOLDSMITH, genteel itinerant, who supported her aged and impoverished parents by traveling from house to house in the environs of Hamilton, New York, painting portraits of the families who gave her bed and board, until she limned in watercolors the likeness of one

George Throop, who married her, therewith terminating her travels and leading to her premature decease, at twenty-seven.

BLESS MRS. AUSTIN ERNEST of Paris, Illinois, whose husband, a local politician of no other fame, organized in 1853 a rally for the Presidential candidate of the new Republican party, following which she gathered the material used to decorate the stand wherefrom the immortal Lincoln spoke and, with scissors and needle and reverential heart, transformed it into a quilted patchwork treasure.

BLESS MARY ANN WILLSON, who in 1810 appeared in the frontier town of Greenville, New York, with her "romantic attachment," a Miss Brundage, with whom she settled in a log cabin, sharing their lives and their gifts, Miss Brundage farming the land, Miss Willson painting dramatic scenes with a bold hand, in colors derived from berries, brickdust, and store paint, and offering her compositions for sale as "rare and unique works of art."

BLESS HANNAH COHOON, who dwelt in the Shaker "City of Peace," Hancock, Massachusetts, where a spirit visited her, as frequently happened there, and gave her "a draft of a beautiful Tree pencil'd on a large sheet of white paper," which she copied out, not knowing till later, with assistance from the Beyond, that it was the Tree of Life; and who saw in another vision, which she likewise reproduced, the Elders of the community feasting on cakes at a table beneath mulberry trees; and who believed, according to the faith of the followers of Mother Ann Lee, that Christ would return to earth in female form.

BLESS IN A CONGREGATION, because they are so numerous, those industrious schoolgirls stitching their alphabets; and the deft ones with needles at lacework, crewel, knitting; and mistresses of spinning, weaving, dyeing; and daughters of tinsmiths painting their ornamental mottoes; and hoarders of rags hooking and braiding their rugs; and adepts in cutouts, valentines, stencils, still lifes, and "fancy pieces"; and middleaged housewives painting, for the joy of it, landscapes and portraits; and makers of bedcovers with names that sing in the night—Rose of Sharon, Princess Feather, Delectable Mountains, Turkey Tracks, Drunkard's Path, Indiana Puzzle, Broken Dishes, Star of LeMoyne, Currants and Coxcomb, Rocky-Road-to-Kansas.

BLESS THEM AND GREET THEM as they pass from their long obscurity, through the gate that separates us from our history, a moving rainbow-cloud of witnesses in a rising hubbub, jubilantly turning to greet one another, this tumult of sisters.

THE CATCH

It darted across the pond
toward our sunset perch,
weaving in, up, and around
a spindle of air,
this delicate engine
fired by impulse and glitter,
swift darning-needle,
gossamer dragon,
less image than thought,
and the thought come alive.
Swoosh went the net
with a practiced hand.
"Da-da, may I look too?"
You may look, child,
all you want.
This prize belongs to no one.
But you will pay all
your life for the privilege,
all your life.

THE CRYSTAL CAGE

for Joseph Cornell

To climb the belltower,
step after step,
in the grainy light,
without breathing harder;
to spy on each landing
a basket of gifts,
a snowbox of wonders:
pressed flowers, pieces
of colored glass,
a postcard from Niagara Falls,
agates, cut-outs of birds,
and dozing in the pile,
in faded mezzotint,
Child Mozart at the Clavichord.
Three days you fasted
to bring you angels;
your square-toed shoes,
friends of your plodding,
are turning weightless.
When the pear-shaped, brindled cat
who lives under the belfry
jumps into your arms
you are not surprised
by the love-look in her amber eyes,
or by the blissful secrets
she confides to you
in oval, pellucid tones.

What if the iron overhead
suddenly starts pounding?
What if, outside,
a terrible storm is raging?
What if, below,
your twisted brother is calling?

SIGNS AND PORTENTS

1

Jonathan, the last of the giant tortoises
on wind-beaten Saint Helena,
misses his island mate,
who died in a fall from a cliff
a century ago.
He is ancient and crusty,
more lonely than Bonaparte
strutting on the volcanic beach,
reviewing his triumphs.
Lately he has made himself
a deliberate nuisance
to the sporting set
of the British Crown Colony
by butting and upending benches
near the tennis courts
and disrupting croquet games
by sitting on the croquet balls.

2

At the Porch of the Caryatids
on the Acropolis
the noble supportive maidens
are stepping down
from their weathered pedestals,
one by one,
to seek asylum in a museum.

Their places will be taken
by identical synthetic sisters
conditioned to withstand
the high, classic, polluted air.

3

Three thousand years ago
they soaked him in pickling brine,
stuffed his body with resins,
baked him in desert heat.
He was Ramses the Second,
feared by Hittites and Israelites,
the hard Pharaoh of *Exodus*,
colossal as the temples
his minions sweated out of rock.
Paris has him now
on temporary loan.
In the aseptic laboratory
of the Musée de l'Homme,
where he lies in state
for special treatment,
who will cure the old mummy
of the loathsome fire
raging under his bandages?

4

Children at play in a field,
tumbling down a hole
into the pristine Palaeolithic,
showed us the way,
ripped the lid from the grotto.
We sped to the spot on wheels
with our cameras and basket lunches.
Now the bison of Lascaux,
prodded from their centuries
of limestone sleep, are sick.
Clots of a virulent mold
suppurate on their flanks,
emitting a green stain.
We name it *la maladie verte*,
an infection from people.
At the back of our minds
squat figures, whose hairy hands
carried torches and the dream of art
through cheerless labyrinths,
gabble in the shadows.

5

On Twelfth Street in Manhattan,
opposite St. Vincent's Mental Pavilion,
while I was sweeping the sidewalk
of its increment of filth,

deposited by dogs and unleashed humans,
a blue van rolled by
with its sidepanel reading:
WORLD FINISHING AND DYEING COMPANY.
I did not catch the face of the driver.

FIRESTICKS

Conjugations of the verb "to be"
asleep since Adam's fall
wake from bad phosphor dreams
heavy with mineral desire.
Earthstruck they leave
their ferny prints of spines
in beds of stone
and carry private moons
down history's long roads,
gaudy with flags.
The one they walk behind
who's named "I AM"
they chose with spurts of flame
to guide them
like the pillar of a cloud
into the mind's white exile.

THE LINCOLN RELICS

"A Lincoln exhibit on view in the Great Hall makes the 16th President of the United States, born 167 years ago, seem very real. Displayed are the contents of his pockets the night he was assassinated, a miniature portrait never before exhibited, and two great documents from the Library's collections, the Gettysburg Address and the Second Inaugural Address."

—Library of Congress Information Bulletin, February 1976

I

Cold-eyed, in Naples once,
while the congregation swooned,
I watched the liquefaction
of a vial of precious blood,
and wondered only
how the trick was done.
Saint's bones are only bones
to me, but here,
where the stage is set
without a trace of gore,
these relics on display—
watchfob and ivory pocket knife,
a handkerchief of Irish linen,
a button severed from his sleeve—

make a noble, dissolving music
out of homely fife and drum,
and that's miraculous.

2

His innocence was to trust
the better angels of our nature,
even when the Union cracked
and furious blood
ran north and south
along the lines of pillage.
Secession grieved him
like the falling-out of brothers.
After Appomattox he laid
the white flower of forgiving
on Lee's crisp sword.
What was there left for him to do?
When the curtain rose
on *Our American Cousin*
he leaned forward in his chair
toward the last absurdity,
that other laughable country,
for which he was ready with his ransom—
a five-dollar Confederate note
in mint condition, and nine
newspaper accolades
neatly folded in his wallet.

It was time for him now
to try on his gold-rimmed spectacles,
the pair with the sliding temples
mended with a loop of string,
while the demon of the absolute,
who had been skulking in the wings,
leaped into focus,
waving a smoking pistol.

3

In the Great Hall of the Library,
as in a glass aquarium,
Abe Lincoln is swimming around,
dressed to the nines
in his stovepipe hat
and swallowtail coat,
effortlessly swimming,
propelled by sudden little kicks
of his gunboat shoes.
His billowing pockets hang
inside out; he is swimming
around, lighter at each turn,
giddy with loss,
while his memory sifts
to the sticky floor.
He is slipping away from us
into his legend and his fame,

having relinquished, piece by piece,
what he carried next to his skin,
what rocked to his angular stride,
partook of his man-smell,
shared the intimacy of his needs.
Mr. President,
in this Imperial City,
awash in gossip and power,
where marble eats marble
and your office has been defiled,
I saw the piranhas darting
between the rose-veined columns,
avid to strip the flesh
from the Republic's bones.
Has no one told you
how the slow blood leaks
from your secret wound?

4

To be old and to be young
again, inglorious private
in the kitchens of the war
that winter of blackout,
walking by the Potomac
in melancholy khaki,
searching for the prairie star,
westward scanning the horizon

for its eloquent and magnanimous light,
yearning to be touched by its fire:
to be touched again, with the years
swirling at my feet, faces
blowing in the wind
around me where I stand,
withered, in the Great Hall.

5

He steps out from the crowd
with his rawboned, warty look,
a gangling fellow in jeans
next to a plum-colored sari,
and just as suddenly he's gone.
But there's that other one
who's tall and lonely.

MEDITATIONS ON DEATH

—from Giuseppe Ungaretti

I

O sister of the shadow,
blackest in strongest light,
Death, you pursue me.

In a pure garden
innocent desire conceived you
and peace was lost,
pensive death,
on your mouth.

From that moment
I hear you in the mind's flow,
sounding the far depths,
suffering rival of eternity.

Poisonous mother of the ages,
fearful of palpitation
and of solitude,

beauty punished and smiling,
in the drowse of flesh
runaway dreamer,

unsleeping athlete
of our greatness,

when you have tamed me, tell me:
in the melancholy of the living
how long will my shadow fly?

II

Probing the deepest selves
of our unhappy mask
(enclosure of the infinite)
with fanatic blandishment—
the dark vigil of our fathers.

Death, mute word,
riverbed of sand deposited
by the blood,
I hear you singing like a locust
in the darkened rose of reflections.

III

Etcher of the secret wrinkles
in our unhappy mask—
the infinite jest of our fathers.

You, in the deep light,
O confused silence,
insist like the angry locusts.

IV

Clouds took me by the hand.

On the hillside I burn space and time,
like one of your messengers,
like a dream, divine death.

V

You have closed your eyes.

A night is born
full of hidden wounds,

of dead sounds
as of corks
when the nets are let down to the water.

Your hands become a breath
of inviolable distances,
slippery as thoughts,

And that equivocation of the moon
and that gentlest rocking,

if you would lay them on my eyes,
touch the soul.

You are the woman who passes by
like a leaf

leaving an autumn fire in the trees.

VI

O beautiful prey,
night-voice,
your movements
breed a fever.

Only you, demented memory,
could capture freedom.

On your elusive flesh
trembling in clouded mirrors
what crimes, I wonder,
did you not teach me to consummate?

With you, phantoms, I have no reticences,

and my heart is filled with your remorse
when it is day.

THE QUARREL

The word I spoke in anger
weighs less than a parsley seed,
but a road runs through it
that leads to my grave,
that bought-and-paid-for lot
on a salt-sprayed hill in Truro
where the scrub pines
overlook the bay.
Half-way I'm dead enough,
strayed from my own nature
and my fierce hold on life.
If I could cry, I'd cry,
but I'm too old to be
anybody's child.
Liebchen,
with whom should I quarrel
except in the hiss of love,
that harsh, irregular flame?

THE UNQUIET ONES

Years ago I lost
both my parents' addresses.
Father and mother lie
in their neglected cribs,
obscure as moles,
unvisited.
I do not need to summon them.
When I put out the light
I hear them stir, dissatisfied,
in their separate places,
in death as in life
remote from each other,
having no conversation
except in the common ground
of their son's mind.
They slip through narrow crevices
and, suddenly blown tall,
glide into my cave of phantoms,
unwelcome guests, but not
unloved, dark emissaries
of the two-faced god.

MY SISTERS

Who whispered, souls have shapes?
So has the wind, I say.
But I don't know,
I only feel things blow.

I had two sisters once
with long black hair
who walked apart from me
and wrote the history of tears.
Their story's faded with their names,
but the candlelight they carried,
like dancers in a dream,
still flickers on their gowns
as they bend over me
to comfort my night-fears.

Let nothing grieve you,
Sarah and Sophia.
Shush, shush, my dears,
now and forever.

ROUTE SIX

The city squats on my back.
I am heart-sore, stiff-necked,
exasperated. That's why
I slammed the door,
that's why I tell you now,
in every house of marriage
there's room for an interpreter.
Let's jump into the car, honey,
and head straight for the Cape,
where the cock on our housetop crows
that the weather's fair,
and my garden waits for me
to coax it into bloom.
As for those passions left
that flare past understanding,
like bundles of dead letters
out of our previous lives
that amaze us with their fevers,
we can stow them in the rear
along with ziggurats of luggage
and Celia, our transcendental cat,
past-mistress of all languages,
including Hottentot and silence.
We'll drive non-stop till dawn,
and if I grow sleepy at the wheel,
you'll keep me awake by singing
in your bravura Chicago style

Ruth Etting's smoky song,
"Love Me or Leave Me,"
belting out the choices.

Light glazes the eastern sky
over Buzzards Bay.
Celia gyrates upward
like a performing seal,
her glistening nostrils aquiver
to sniff the brine-spiked air.
The last stretch toward home!
Twenty summers roll by.

THE LAYERS

I have walked through many lives,
some of them my own,
and I am not who I was,
though some principle of being
abides, from which I struggle
not to stray.
When I look behind,
as I am compelled to look
before I can gather strength
to proceed on my journey,
I see the milestones dwindling
toward the horizon
and the slow fires trailing
from the abandoned camp-sites,
over which scavenger angels
wheel on heavy wings.
Oh, I have made myself a tribe
out of my true affections,
and my tribe is scattered!
How shall the heart be reconciled
to its feast of losses?
In a rising wind
the manic dust of my friends,
those who fell along the way,
bitterly stings my face.
Yet I turn, I turn,
exulting somewhat,

with my will intact to go
wherever I need to go,
and every stone on the road
precious to me.
In my darkest night,
when the moon was covered
and I roamed through wreckage,
a nimbus-clouded voice
directed me:
"Live in the layers,
not on the litter."
Though I lack the art
to decipher it,
no doubt the next chapter
in my book of transformations
is already written.
I am not done with my changes.

from

Next-to-Last-Things

(1 9 8 5)

THE SNAKES
OF SEPTEMBER

All summer I heard them
rustling in the shrubbery,
outracing me from tier
to tier in my garden,
a whisper among the viburnums,
a signal flashed from the hedgerow,
a shadow pulsing
in the barberry thicket.
Now that the nights are chill
and the annuals spent,
I should have thought them gone,
in a torpor of blood
slipped to the nether world
before the sickle frost.
Not so. In the deceptive balm
of noon, as if defiant of the curse
that spoiled another garden,
these two appear on show
through a narrow slit
in the dense green brocade
of a north-country spruce,
dangling head-down, entwined
in a brazen love-knot.
I put out my hand and stroke
the fine, dry grit of their skins.
After all,

we are partners in this land,
co-signers of a covenant.
At my touch the wild
braid of creation
trembles.

THE ABDUCTION

Some things I do not profess
to understand, perhaps
not wanting to, including
whatever it was they did
with you or you with them
that timeless summer day
when you stumbled out of the wood,
distracted, with your white blouse torn
and a bloodstain on your skirt.
"Do you believe?" you asked.
Between us, through the years,
from bits, from broken clues,
we pieced enough together
to make the story real:
how you encountered on the path
a pack of sleek, grey hounds,
trailed by a dumbshow retinue
in leather shrouds; and how
you were led, through leafy ways,
into the presence of a royal stag,
flaming in his chestnut coat,
who kneeled on a swale of moss
before you; and how you were borne
aloft in triumph through the green,
stretched on his rack of budding horn,

till suddenly you found yourself alone
in a trampled clearing.

That was a long time ago,
almost another age, but even now,
when I hold you in my arms,
I wonder where you are.
Sometimes I wake to hear
the engines of the night thrumming
outside the east bay window
on the lawn spreading to the rose garden.
You lie beside me in elegant repose,
a hint of transport hovering on your lips,
indifferent to the harsh green flares
that swivel through the room,
searchlights controlled by unseen hands.
Out there is childhood country,
bleached faces peering in
with coals for eyes.
Our lives are spinning out
from world to world;
the shapes of things
are shifting in the wind.
What do we know
beyond the rapture and the dread?

RACCOON JOURNAL

July 14
rac-coon', n. from the American Indian (Algonquian)
arahkunem, "he scratches with the hands."
                                    —*New World Dictionary*

July 17

They live promiscuously in the woods
above the marsh, snuggling in hollow trees
or rock-piled hillside dens,
from which they swagger in dead of night,
nosy, precocious, bushy-tailed,
to inspect their properties in town.

At every house they drop a calling card,
doorstep deposits of soft reddish scats
and heavy sprays of territorial scent
that on damp mornings mixes with the dew.

August 21–26

I've seen them, under the streetlight,
paddling up the lane,
five pelts in single file,
halting in unison to topple
a garbage can and gorge
on lobster shells and fish heads
or scattered parts of chicken.

Last year my neighbor's dog,
a full-grown Labrador retriever,
chased a grizzly old codger
into the tidal basin,
where shaggy arms reached up
from the ooze to embrace him,
dragging his muzzle under
until at length he drowned.

There's nobody left this side
of Gull Hill to tangle
with them, certainly not
my superannuated cat,
domesticated out of nature,
who stretches by the stove
and puts on a show of bristling.
She does that even when mice
go racing round the kitchen.
We seem to be two of a kind,
though that's not to say I'm happy
paying my vegetable tithe
over and over
out of ripe summer's bounty
to feed omnivorous appetites,
or listening to the scratch of prowlers
from the fragrant terraces, as they
dig-dig-dig, because they're mad

for bonemeal, uprooting plants and bulbs,
whole clumps, squirming and dank,
wherever they catch a whiff
of buried angel dust.

October 31

To be like Orpheus, who could talk
with animals in their own language:
in sleep I had that art, but now
I've waked into the separate
wilderness of age,
where the old, libidinous beasts
assume familiar shapes,
pretending to be tamed.

Raccoons! I can hear them
confabulating on the porch,
half-churring, half-growling,
bubbling to a manic hoot
that curdles the night-air.
Something out there appalls.
On the back door screen
a heavy furpiece hangs,
spreadeagled, breathing hard,
hooked by prehensile fingers,
with its pointed snout pressing in,
and the dark agates of its bandit eyes

furiously blazing. Behind,
where shadows deepen, burly forms
lumber from side to side
like diminished bears
in a flatfooted shuffle.
They watch me, unafraid.
I know they'll never leave,
they've come to take possession.

Provincetown 1984

THE OLD DARNED MAN

Back in the thirties, in the midst of the Depression, I fled the city and moved to a Connecticut farm. It was the period of my first marriage. We lived in an old gambrel house, built about 1740, on top of a ridge called Wormwood Hill. I had bought the house, together with more than 100 acres of woodland and pasture, for $500 down. It had no electricity, no heat, no running water, and it was in bad repair, but it was a great, beautiful house. I spent most of three years, working with my hands, making it habitable. At that time early American art and furniture were practically being given away. Poor as we were, we managed to fill the house with priceless stuff. We were so far from the city and from all signs of progress that we might as well have been living in another age.

One spring there appeared on the road, climbing up the hill, a man in a patchwork suit, with a battered silk hat on his head. His trousers and swallow-tail coat had been mended so many times, with varicolored swatches, that when he approached us, over the brow of the hill, he looked like a crazy-quilt on stilts.

He was an itinerant tinker, dried-out and old, thin as a scarecrow, with a high, cracked voice. He asked for pots and pans to repair, scissors and knives to sharpen. In the shade of the sugar maples, that a colonel in Washington's army was said to have planted, he set up his shop and silently went to work on the articles I handed to him.

When he was done, I offered him lunch in the kitchen. He would not sit down to eat, but accepted some food in a bag.

"I have been here before," he said to me quietly. On our way out, while we were standing in the front hall at the foot of the staircase, he suddenly cried, "I hear the worms tumbling in this house." "What do you mean?" I asked. He did not answer, but cupped his hands over his eyes. I took it as a bad omen, a fateful prophecy, about my house, my marriage. And so it turned out to be.

Some time later I learned that my visitor was a legendary figure, known throughout the countryside as the Old Darned Man. He had been a brilliant divinity student at Yale, engaged to a childhood sweetheart, with the wedding set for the day after graduation. But on that very day, while he waited at the church, the news was brought to him that she had run off with his dearest friend. Ever since then he had been wandering distractedly from village to village in his wedding clothes.

As for the worms, they belonged to a forgotten page in local history. Late in the nineteenth century the housewives of the region, dreaming of a fortune to be made, had started a cottage industry in silkworm culture, importing the worms from China. The parlors of every farmhouse were lined with stacks of silkworm trays, in which the worms munched on mulberry leaves, making clicking and whispering noises. That was the sound heard in my hall.

It's a story without a happy ending. The worms died; the dreams of riches faded; abandoned plows rusted in the farmyards; one breathless summer day a black-funneled twister wheeled up Wormwood Hill from the stricken valley, dismantling my house, my barn, my grove of sugar maples; the face of my bride darkened and broke into a wild laughter; I never saw the Old Darned Man again.

THE SCENE

—after Alexander Blok

Night. Street. Lamp. Drugstore.
A world of dim and sleazy light.
You may live twenty-five years more.
Nothing will change. No way out.

You die. You're born again and all
Will be repeated as before:
The cold ripple of a canal.
Night. Street. Lamp. Drugstore.

THE IMAGE-MAKER

A wind passed over my mind,
insidious and cold.
It is a thought, I thought,
but it was only its shadow.
Words came,
or the breath of my sisters,
with a black rustle of wings.
They came with a summons
that followed a blessing.
I could not believe
I too would be punished.
Perhaps it is time to go,
to slip alone, as at a birth,
out of this glowing house
where all my children danced.
Seductive Night! I have stood
at my casement the longest hour,
watching the acid wafer
of the moon slowly dissolving
in a scud of cloud, and heard
the farthest hidden stars
calling my name.
I listen, but I avert my ears
from Meister Eckhart's warning:
All things must be forsaken.
God scorns
to show Himself among images.

LAMPLIGHTER: 1914

What I remember most was not
the incident at Sarajevo,
but the first flying steamkettle
puffing round the bend,
churning up the dirt
between the rocky pastures
as it came riding high
on its red wheels
in a blare of shining brass;
and my bay stallion snorting,
rearing in fright, bolting,
leaving me sprawled on the ground;
and our buggy
careening out of sight,
those loose reins dangling,
racing toward its rendezvous
with Hammond's stone wall
in an explosion of wood and flesh,
the crack of smashed cannon bones.
Who are these strangers
sprung out of the fields?
It is my friend, almost my brother,
who points a gun
to the crooked head.

Once I was a lamplighter
on the Quinnapoxet roads,

making the rounds with Prince,
who was older than I and knew
by heart each of our stations,
needing no whoa of command
nor a tug at his bridle.
That was the summer I practiced
sleight-of-hand and fell asleep
over my picture-books of magic.
Toward dusk, at crossings
and at farmhouse gates,
under the solitary iron trees
I stood on the rim of the buggy wheel
and raised my enchanter's wand,
with its tip of orange flame,
to the gas mantles in their cages,
touching them, one by one,
till the whole countryside bloomed.

DAY OF FOREBODING

Great events are about to happen.
I have seen migratory birds
in unprecedented numbers
descend on the coastal plain,
picking the margins clean.
My bones are a family in their tent
huddled over a small fire
waiting for the uncertain signal
to resume the long march.

THREE SMALL PARABLES FOR
MY POET FRIENDS

I

Certain saurian species, notably the skink, are capable of shedding their tails in self-defense when threatened. The detached appendage diverts attention to itself by taking on a life of its own and thrashing furiously about. As soon as the stalking wildcat pounces on the wriggler, snatching it up from the sand to bite and maul it, the free lizard scampers off. A new tail begins to grow in place of the one that has been sacrificed.

2

The larva of the tortoise beetle has the neat habit of collecting its droppings and exfoliated skin into a little packet that it carries over its back when it is out in the open. If it were not for this fecal shield, it would lie naked before its enemies.

3

Among the Bedouins, the beggar poets of the desert are held in contempt because of their greed, their thievery and venality. Everyone in the scattered encampments knows that poems of praise can be bought, even by the worst of scoundrels, for food or money. Furthermore, these wandering minstrels are notorious for stealing the ideas, lines, and even whole songs of others. Often the recitation is interrupted by the shouts of the squatters around the campfire: "Thou liest. Thou stolest it from So-and-so!" When the poet tries to defend himself, calling for witnesses to vouch for his probity or, in extremity, appealing to Allah, his hearers hoot him down, crying, "Kassad, kaddab! A poet is a liar."

THE ROUND

Light splashed this morning
on the shell-pink anemones
swaying on their tall stems;
down blue-spiked veronica
light flowed in rivulets
over the humps of the honeybees;
this morning I saw light kiss
the silk of the roses
in their second flowering,
my late bloomers
flushed with their brandy.
A curious gladness shook me.

So I have shut the doors of my house,
so I have trudged downstairs to my cell,
so I am sitting in semi-dark
hunched over my desk
with nothing for a view
to tempt me
but a bloated compost heap,
steamy old stinkpile,
under my window;
and I pick my notebook up
and I start to read aloud
the still-wet words I scribbled

on the blotted page:
"Light splashed . . ."

I can scarcely wait till tomorrow
when a new life begins for me,
as it does each day,
as it does each day.

PASSING THROUGH

—on my seventy-ninth birthday

Nobody in the widow's household
ever celebrated anniversaries.
In the secrecy of my room
I would not admit I cared
that my friends were given parties.
Before I left town for school
my birthday went up in smoke
in a fire at City Hall that gutted
the Department of Vital Statistics.
If it weren't for a census report
of a five-year-old White Male
sharing my mother's address
at the Green Street tenement in Worcester
I'd have no documentary proof
that I exist. You are the first,
my dear, to bully me
into these festive occasions.

Sometimes, you say, I wear
an abstracted look that drives you
up the wall, as though it signified
distress or disaffection.
Don't take it so to heart.
Maybe I enjoy not-being as much
as being who I am. Maybe
it's time for me to practice
growing old. The way I look

at it, I'm passing through a phase:
gradually I'm changing to a word.
Whatever you choose to claim
of me is always yours;
nothing is truly mine
except my name. I only
borrowed this dust.

THE LONG BOAT

When his boat snapped loose
from its moorings, under
the screaking of the gulls,
he tried at first to wave
to his dear ones on shore,
but in the rolling fog
they had already lost their faces.
Too tired even to choose
between jumping and calling,
somehow he felt absolved and free
of his burdens, those mottoes
stamped on his name-tag:
conscience, ambition, and all
that caring.
He was content to lie down
with the family ghosts
in the slop of his cradle,
buffeted by the storm,
endlessly drifting.
Peace! Peace!
To be rocked by the Infinite!
As if it didn't matter
which way was home;
as if he didn't know
he loved the earth so much
he wanted to stay forever.

THE WELLFLEET WHALE

*A few summers ago, on Cape Cod, a whale foundered on the beach,
a sixty-three-foot finback whale. When the tide went out, I approached
him. He was lying there, in monstrous desolation, making the most
terrifying noises—rumbling—groaning. I put my hands on his flanks
and I could feel the life inside him. And while I was standing there,
suddenly he opened his eye. It was a big, red, cold eye, and it was
staring directly at me. A shudder of recognition passed between us.
Then the eye closed forever. I've been thinking about whales ever since.*

—Journal entry

I

You have your language too,
 an eerie medley of clicks
  and hoots and trills,
location-notes and love calls,
  whistles and grunts. Occasionally,
   it's like furniture being smashed,
or the creaking of a mossy door,
  sounds that all melt into a liquid
   song with endless variations,
as if to compensate
 for the vast loneliness of the sea.
  Sometimes a disembodied voice
breaks in as if from distant reefs,
  and it's as much as one can bear
   to listen to its long mournful cry,

a sorrow without name, both more
    and less than human. It drags
        across the ear like a record
running down.

2

No wind. No waves. No clouds.
    Only the whisper of the tide,
        as it withdrew, stroking the shore,
a lazy drift of gulls overhead,
    and tiny points of light
        bubbling in the channel.
It was the tag-end of summer.
    From the harbor's mouth
        you coasted into sight,
flashing news of your advent,
    the crescent of your dorsal fin
        clipping the diamonded surface.
We cheered at the sign of your greatness
    when the black barrel of your head
        erupted, ramming the water,
and you flowered for us
    in the jet of your spouting.

3

All afternoon you swam
    tirelessly round the bay,
        with such an easy motion,

the slightest downbeat of your tail,
  an almost imperceptible
    undulation of your flippers,
you seemed like something poured,
  not driven; you seemed
    to marry grace with power.
And when you bounded into air,
  slapping your flukes,
    we thrilled to look upon
pure energy incarnate
  as nobility of form.
    You seemed to ask of us
not sympathy, or love,
  or understanding,
    but awe and wonder.

That night we watched you
  swimming in the moon.
    Your back was molten silver.
We guessed your silent passage
  by the phosphorescence in your wake.
    At dawn we found you stranded on the rocks.

4

There came a boy and a man
  and yet other men running, and two
    schoolgirls in yellow halters

and a housewife bedecked
   with curlers, and whole families in beach
      buggies with assorted yelping dogs.
The tide was almost out.
   We could walk around you,
      as you heaved deeper into the shoal,
crushed by your own weight,
   collapsing into yourself,
      your flippers and your flukes
quivering, your blowhole
   spasmodically bubbling, roaring.
      In the pit of your gaping mouth
you bared your fringework of baleen,
   a thicket of horned bristles.
      When the Curator of Mammals
arrived from Boston
   to take samples of your blood
      you were already oozing from below.
Somebody had carved his initials
   in your flank. Hunters of souvenirs
      had peeled off strips of your skin,
a membrane thin as paper.
   You were blistered and cracked by the sun.
      The gulls had been pecking at you.
The sound you made was a hoarse and fitful bleating.

What drew us, like a magnet, to your dying?
　　You made a bond between us,
　　　　the keepers of the nightfall watch,
who gathered in a ring around you,
　　boozing in the bonfire light.
　　　　Toward dawn we shared with you
your hour of desolation,
　　the huge lingering passion
　　　　of your unearthly outcry,
as you swung your blind head
　　toward us and laboriously opened
　　　　a bloodshot, glistening eye,
in which we swam with terror and recognition.

5

Voyager, chief of the pelagic world,
　　you brought with you the myth
　　　　of another country, dimly remembered,
where flying reptiles
　　lumbered over the steaming marshes
　　　　and trumpeting thunder lizards
wallowed in the reeds.
　　While empires rose and fell on land,
　　　　your nation breasted the open main,
rocked in the consoling rhythm
　　of the tides. Which ancestor first plunged
　　　　head-down through zones of colored twilight

to scour the bottom of the dark?
   You ranged the North Atlantic track
     from Port-of-Spain to Baffin Bay,
edging between the ice-floes
   through the fat of summer,
     lob-tailing, breaching, sounding,
grazing in the pastures of the sea
   on krill-rich orange plankton
     crackling with life.
You prowled down the continental shelf,
   guided by the sun and stars
     and the taste of alluvial silt
on your way southward
   to the warm lagoons,
     the tropic of desire,
where the lovers lie belly to belly
   in the rub and nuzzle of their sporting;
     and you turned, like a god in exile,
out of your wide primeval element,
   delivered to the mercy of time.

   Master of the whale-roads,
let the white wings of the gulls
   spread out their cover.
   You have become like us,
disgraced and mortal.

New Poems

MY MOTHER'S PEARS

Plump, green-gold, Worcester's pride,
  transported through autumn skies
    in a box marked Handle With Care

sleep eighteen Bartlett pears,
  hand-picked and polished and packed
    for deposit at my door,

each in its crinkled nest
  with a stub of stem attached
    and a single bright leaf like a flag.

A smaller than usual crop,
  but still enough to share with me,
    as always at harvest time.

Those strangers are my friends
  whose kindness blesses the house
    my mother built at the edge of town

beyond the last trolley-stop
  when the century was young, and she
    proposed, for her children's sake,

to marry again, not knowing how soon
  the windows would grow dark
    and the velvet drapes come down.

Rubble accumulates in the yard,
    workmen are hammering on the roof,
        I am standing knee-deep in dirt

with a shovel in my hand.
    Mother has wrapped a kerchief round her head,
        her glasses glint in the sun.

When my sisters appear on the scene,
    gangly and softly tittering,
        she waves them back into the house

to fetch us pails of water,
    and they skip out of our sight
        in their matching middy blouses.

I summon up all my strength
    to set the pear tree in the ground,
        unwinding its burlap shroud.

It is taller than I. "Make room
    for the roots!" my mother cries,
        "Dig the hole deeper."

CHARIOT

In this image of my friend's studio,
where curiosity runs the shop, and you
can almost smell the nostalgic dust
settling on the junk of lost mythologies,
the artist himself stays out of view.
Yet anyone could guess
this is the magician's place
from his collection of conical hats
and the sprawled puppets on a shelf,
the broken as well as the whole,
that have grown to resemble him,
or the other way round.
Butterflies, gameboards, and bells,
strewn jacks and alphabet blocks,
spindles, old music scores—
the litter spreads from wall to wall.
If you could dig to the bottom,
you might expect to find
a child's plush heart,
a shining agate eye.
Here everything waits to be renewed.
That horse-age wagon wheel
propped in the corner
against an empty picture-frame,
even in its state of disrepair,
minus three spokes,

looks poised for flight.
Tomorrow, maybe, at the crack of a whip
a flock of glittering birds will perch
on its rim, a burnished stranger
wearing an enigmatic mask
will mount its hub
and the great battered wheel
will start to spin.

IN THE DARK HOUSE

"The injury cannot be healed; it extends through time, and the Furies, in whose existence we are forced to believe . . . perpetuate the tormentor's work by denying peace to the tormented."

—Primo Levi

People had celebrated him as a god
because his art, they said, was magical,
sweeter to them than the soft spring rains
that blew off the lilac mountains,
secret as the wind whispering through the olives.
Eurydice, his lissome bride!
He made a caressing music
out of the vowels of her name.
All that he ever wanted was to sing of his love.

Where had they gone, that ragtag minstrel band,
those merry dancers, with whom he strolled
at the green earth's invitation,
their ranks swelling at each crossroad?
How young they were
who crowned him king of their carnival!
And the news raced ahead that at his passing
trees broke into blossom out of season,
nightingales and owls perched on his shoulders,
and down the winding country roads
processions of wild beasts,
great spotted cats, weasels, and wolves
tagged meekly at his heels, tamed by his song.

If he could reinvent those melting chords
struck from his nights of loneliness and need
that won reprieve in Hades' rancid halls,
would he rejoice again to see
the dark lord shed a cold, permissive tear?

He dared not look behind, nor could he guess
how distantly she trailed: that was the Law,
senseless and cruel, but still
the Law, imposing separate silences
on two who struggled up the fetid slope,
gasping for breath, through swirls of sulphur clouds
that parted to reveal, in oozing light,
covens of Harpies roosting on the walls,
and smoldering on the rock-strewn course ahead
bonfires that seemed to plead with writhing arms.

At the blackened gate, a single step removed
from sunlight, birdcalls, and the heady air
he waited for her to join him
and to catch his hand, perhaps to murmur
the lost, impetuous, redemptive word.
Instead he heard her shrill, inhuman wail,
a tunnel-echo locked into his ears,
the cry of souls unsuited for this life,
having been touched by evil past forgiveness.

Yes, he had turned, as anybody would,
as certainly she knew he would, and saw her,
in that instant she was whisked away,
clawing at the shawl that hid her from the world
to show him the ravaged face of all farewells
and the blank pennies of her defeated eyes.

As he sat in the dark, in the shuttered house,
Orpheus heard the women hooting in the street
outside, raving against him, blaming him
for their sister's loss. Apollo's priceless gift
lay dusty at his feet, so much a part of him
he wondered why its strings did not crack for grief.
How could he deny that frenzied mob,
not to be assuaged except by blood,
when his own heart cried worse?
He listened for the trampling on the stairs.

HALLEY'S COMET

Miss Murphy in first grade
wrote its name in chalk
across the board and told us
it was roaring down the stormtracks
of the Milky Way at frightful speed
and if it wandered off its course
and smashed into the earth
there'd be no school tomorrow.
A red-bearded preacher from the hills
with a wild look in his eyes
stood in the public square
at the playground's edge
proclaiming he was sent by God
to save every one of us,
even the little children.
"Repent, ye sinners!" he shouted,
waving his hand-lettered sign.
At supper I felt sad to think
that it was probably
the last meal I'd share
with my mother and my sisters;
but I felt excited too
and scarcely touched my plate.
So mother scolded me
and sent me early to my room.
The whole family's asleep
except for me. They never heard me steal

into the stairwell hall and climb
the ladder to the fresh night air.

Look for me, Father, on the roof
of the red brick building
at the foot of Green Street—
that's where we live, you know, on the top floor.
I'm the boy in the white flannel gown
sprawled on this coarse gravel bed
searching the starry sky,
waiting for the world to end.

HORNWORM:
SUMMER REVERIE

Here in caterpillar country
I learned how to survive
by pretending to be a dragon.
See me put on that look
of slow and fierce surprise
when I lift my bulbous head
and glare at an intruder.
Nobody seems to guess
how gentle I really am,
content most of the time
simply to disappear
by melting into the scenery.
Smooth and fatty and long,
with seven white stripes
painted on either side
and a sharp little horn for a tail,
I lie stretched out on a leaf,
pale green on my bed of green,
munching, munching.

HORNWORM:
AUTUMN LAMENTATION

Since that first morning when I crawled
into the world, a naked grubby thing,
and found the world unkind,
my dearest faith has been that this
is but a trial: I shall be changed.
In my imaginings I have already spent
my brooding winter underground,
unfolded silky powdered wings, and climbed
into the air, free as a puff of cloud
to sail over the steaming fields,
alighting anywhere I pleased,
thrusting into deep tubular flowers.

It is not so: there may be nectar
in those cups, but not for me.
All day, all night, I carry on my back
embedded in my flesh, two rows
of little white cocoons,
so neatly stacked
they look like eggs in a crate.
And I am eaten half away.

If I can gather strength enough
I'll try to burrow under a stone
and spin myself a purse
in which to sleep away the cold;
though when the sun kisses the earth

again, I know I won't be there.
Instead, out of my chrysalis
will break, like robbers from a tomb,
a swarm of parasitic flies,
leaving my wasted husk behind.

Sir, you with the red snippers
in your hand, hovering over me,
casting your shadow, I greet you,
whether you come as an angel of death
or of mercy. But tell me,
before you choose to slice me in two:
Who can understand the ways
of the Great Worm in the Sky?

THE SEA, THAT HAS NO ENDING . . .

"*Green Sea* is one of a series of paintings [Philip] Guston did in
1976 featuring a tangle of disembodied legs, bent at the knees and
wearing flat, ungainly shoes, grouped on the horizon of a deep green
sea against a salmon-colored backdrop . . . Its meaning eludes us."
      —descriptive note, Master Paintings in the Art Institute
      of Chicago

Who are we? Why are we here,
huddled on this desolate shore,
so curiously chopped and joined?—
broken totems, a scruffy tribe!
How many years have passed
since we owned keys to a door,
had friends, walked down familiar streets
and answered to a name? We try
not to remember the places
where we left pieces of ourselves
along the way, whether in ditches
at the side of foreign roads
or under signs that spell "For Hire"
or naked between the sheets in cheap
motels. Does anybody care?
All the villagers have fled
from the sorry sight of us.
In the beginning we had faith
that the Master, who day and night
lets nothing escape the glare
from his invisible tower,

would soften at our appeals;
but we are baffled by his replies
even more than by his silences.
When we complain of the cruel sun
and the blisters popping in our skin
he turns our suffering against us:
A great wound, one you could claim
your very own, might have saved you.
Instead you let others do you in
with their small knives.
What is to become of us?
The sea, that has no ending,
is lapping at our feet.
How we long for the cleansing waters
to rise and cover us forever!
But he who reads our secret thoughts
rebukes us, saying: *You cannot hope*
to be restored unless you dare
to plunge head-down into the mystery
and there confront the beasts
that prowl on the ocean floor.
"Sacred monsters" is what he calls them.
If only we had strength enough
or nerve for a grand heroic action.
Habit has made it easier for us
to wait for the blessing of the tide.
It's really strange how much we miss

those people who came to gape and jeer;
we'd welcome their return, for company.
Why is the Master knocking at our ears,
demanding immediate attention?
In the acid of his voice we sense
the horns swelling at his temples
and little drops of spittle
bubbling at the corners of his mouth.
This is not an exhibition, he storms,
it's a life!

PROTEUS

At midday he rose on schedule from the flood
to stretch his limbs on the kelp-strewn shelf
of rock, where he could soak his bones
in the drippings of the sun
and watch, bemused, the monsters of the deep,
who were his sacred charge,
humping and snorting at their brutish games.

He was not envious of their rampant blood,
nor had he bargained for this keeper's role.
Their origins were buried in his past,
lost syllables in a language of forgetting.
Perhaps they were his misbegotten brood,
conceived by night in another age, but why
should he be vexed, as in his wanton prime,
by buzzing guilts and blames, that cloud of flies?
His burden was to see the future plain.

On shore, he knew, under the beetling crags
lurked bands of marauders in their painted skins,
waiting for him to lapse into a drowse,
when they would pounce upon him in repose
and pin him down, compelling him
to rip the sweating membrane from the void
and practice his excruciating art.

He was the world's supreme illusionist,
taught by necessity how to melt his cage,

slipping at will through his adversaries' grasp
by self-denial, displaying one by one
his famous repertoire of shifting forms,
from lion and serpent to fire and waterfall.
But now he was heavy in his heart, and languid,
sensing the time had come to leave his flock.
Must he prepare himself once more for the test?
He could not recollect the secret codes
that gave him access to his other lives.

Half-listening to the plashing of the oars,
a disembodied chorus from the sea,
he shut his dimming eyes
and did not stir. These were the dreaded boatmen
racing to his side, and these their hairy hands.
He heard barbaric voices crying, "Prophesy!"

TOUCH ME

Summer is late, my heart.
Words plucked out of the air
some forty years ago
when I was wild with love
and torn almost in two
scatter like leaves this night
of whistling wind and rain.
It is my heart that's late,
it is my song that's flown.
Outdoors all afternoon
under a gunmetal sky
staking my garden down,
I kneeled to the crickets trilling
underfoot as if about
to burst from their crusty shells;
and like a child again
marveled to hear so clear
and brave a music pour
from such a small machine.
What makes the engine go?
Desire, desire, desire.
The longing for the dance
stirs in the buried life.
One season only,
                    and it's done.
So let the battered old willow

thrash against the windowpanes
and the house timbers creak.
Darling, do you remember
the man you married? Touch me,
remind me who I am.

NOTES

THE TESTING-TREE

JOURNAL FOR MY DAUGHTER. Written during the period of
student rebellion and mass demonstrations provoked by the
Vietnam War. The "uncle-bear" in Part 5 is an evocation of
Theodore Roethke on one of his visits in the early fifties.

AN OLD CRACKED TUNE. The first line is borrowed from an
odious street song about a Jewish tailor that I recall from my
student days in the twenties.

THE MAGIC CURTAIN. Frieda's song (literal translation):
    One, two, three, four, five, six, seven,
    what has become of my beloved?
    He is not here, he is not there.
    He's gone away to America.

AFTER THE LAST DYNASTY. Chairman Mao's summation of his
strategy of guerrilla warfare: "Enemy advances, we retreat;
enemy halts, we harass; enemy tires, we attack; enemy retreats,
we pursue."

RIVER ROAD. Location: New Hope, Bucks County, Pennsylvania,
where I lived for several years prior to my departure in 1941
for military service in World War II.

TRISTIA. Mandelstam's Latin title, signifying Poems of Sorrow,
alludes to the elegiac epistles of Ovid, which the Roman poet

began on his journey into exile in Tomis, a Black Sea outpost. Ovid spoke of the sorrow of exile, of his unconquerable will to survive and to write, of his loves, and of his hope that he might be allowed to return to Rome. Mandelstam (1891–1938) never returned from the prison camp to which Stalin sent him.

THE MOUND BUILDERS. The civilization of the Mound Builders, of whom regrettably little is known, flourished between A.D. 900 and 1100. The site of their community in Georgia was later held sacred by the Creek Nation. At the time of my visit to the Ocmulgee National Monument, in the spring of 1962, President Kennedy had just announced the resumption of nuclear testing by the United States.

THE GLADIATORS. The impulsive monk who tried to stop the bloodshed suffered his martyrdom at the hands of the enraged spectators about A.D. 400. The scandal of his dismemberment led to the proscription of man-to-man combats. In actual historical sequence, which I have telescoped, the barbarous Children's Crusades did not eventuate till the thirteenth century.

AROUND PASTOR BONHOEFFER. Dietrich Bonhoeffer was a German Lutheran pastor and theologian whose Christian conscience forced him, against the pacific temper of his spirit, to accept the necessity of political activism and to join in a conspiracy for the murder of Hitler. The plot failed, and he was arrested by the Gestapo (1943). On April 9, 1945, he was hanged at Flossenburg extermination camp. His brother Klaus and two brothers-in-law were also destroyed. Some of the details of the poem have their source in Bonhoeffer's two posthumous publications, *The Cost of Discipleship* and *Letters and Papers from Prison*, and in the biography by his disciple Eberhard Bethge.

BOLSHEVIKS. Aba Stolzenberg (1905–1941) was an obscure Yiddish poet who came to the United States from Poland. Irving Howe, in the course of compiling *A Treasury of Yiddish Poetry* (Holt, Rinehart and Winston, 1969) in collaboration with Eliezer Greenberg, introduced me to Stolzenberg's work and provided me with a transliteration of the text.

THE FLIGHT OF APOLLO. Written on the occasion of the flight of Apollo 11 and the first lunar landing, July 20, 1969.

KING OF THE RIVER. Within two weeks after leaving the ocean to swim up the rivers of the Northwest and spawn, the bounding Pacific salmon degenerates into an aged, colorless, and almost lifeless fish. The same geriatric process in humans takes some twenty to forty years.

CLEOPATRA, DANTE, BORIS PASTERNAK. Anna Akhmatova (1888–1966), friend and peer of Pasternak and Mandelstam, is one of the heroic figures of modern Russian poetry. During the Stalin Terror, her loved ones were killed or imprisoned and she herself was vilified, censored, and silenced. Like Dante in her poem, she refused to play the part of the humble penitent. In her tribute to Pasternak she plaits a garland for him out of favorite images from his work.

The Daryal Gorge runs through the Caucasus into Georgia, which Pasternak often visited in the thirties to see his friends, the poets Paolo Yashvili and Titsian Tabidze, both of whom were to die in the purges.

I am indebted to the late Max Hayward, fellow of St. Antony's College, Oxford, for his renderings of the Russian texts and his invaluable commentaries. Our close collaboration for several years led to the publication of *Poems of Akhmatova* (Atlantic-Little, Brown) in 1973.

THE ARTIST. Written following the suicide in New York of my friend the painter Mark Rothko, on February 25, 1970.

THE TESTING-TREE. When I was a boy in Worcester, Massachusetts, my family lived on top of a hill, at the thin edge of the city, with the woods beyond. Much of the time I was alone, but I learned how not to be lonely, exploring the surrounding fields and the old Indian trails. In the games that I improvised, most of them involved with running, climbing, and a variety of ball-skills, I was a fierce competitor, representing in turn myself and my imaginary opponent. It did not occur to me to be surprised that "I" was always the winner.

The stone-throwing that figures in the poem was of a somewhat special order, since it did more than try my skill: it challenged destiny. My life hinged on the three throws permitted me, according to my rules. If I hit the target-oak once, somebody would love me; if I hit it twice, I should be a poet; if I scored all three times, I should never die. A friend of mine tells me that what I have recorded here is recognizable as an ancient ritual, and that the patriarchal scarred oak, as I have described it, is transparently a manifestation of the King of the Wood. Such mysteries for a Worcester childhood!

THE LAYERS

WHAT OF THE NIGHT? Several of the details in Part 2 derive from Franz Kafka's story "The Country Doctor."

QUINNAPOXET. Quinnapoxet (sometimes spelled with one *n*) was a backwater village, no longer in existence, outside Worcester, Massachusetts, where I spent many of my childhood summers as a boarder on the Buteau family farm. The poem came to me in a dream.

WORDS FOR THE UNKNOWN MAKERS. Rose Slivka, then editor of the periodical *Craft Horizons*, gave me *carte blanche* to write on the unprecedented exhibition "The Flowering of American Folk Art 1776–1876," at the Whitney Museum of American Art, New York, February 1 to March 24, 1974. This suite of poems, with photographic illustrations from the exhibition, appeared in the February 1974 issue of *Craft Horizons*.

TO A SLAVE NAMED JOB. "Job's Cigar Store Indian," in polychromed wood, is believed to have been made by a slave (c. 1825) for a tobacconist in Freehold, New Jersey.

SACRED TO THE MEMORY. Based on an unsigned watercolor, "Mourning Picture for Polly Botsford and Her Children," painted c. 1813 and found in Connecticut.

TROMPE L'OEIL. Several nineteenth-century country artisans became masters of illusion, developing techniques that enabled them to simulate, on ordinary pine, the inlays, veneers, and graining of expensive furniture.

A BLESSING OF WOMEN. Jean Lipman and Alice Winchester, who organized the Whitney exhibition and made a book out of it, provided the biographical information incorporated into this poem. See *The Flowering of American Folk Art, 1776–1876* (Viking Press, 1974).

THE CRYSTAL CAGE. Contributed, together with my original collage, to Dore Ashton's *A Joseph Cornell Album* (Viking Press, 1974). My title is taken from one of Cornell's early boxes.

Signs and Portents. Since this poem was written in 1976–1977, Ramses II has been returned to Egypt from Paris after treatment for his infection; the delicate operation of removing the Caryatids from the Erectheum has been completed; the Caves of Lascaux are open again to visitors, but on a limited basis; no further word has reached me from Saint Helena about the fate of Jonathan the giant tortoise.

Firesticks. For José Guerrero (1914–1991). Originally published in a portfolio with related serigraphs by the Spanish-born painter: *Fosforencias*, by José Guerrero (Galeria Juana Mordo, Madrid, and El Museo de Arte Abstracto Español, Cuenca, 1971).

The Lincoln Relics. The exhibition of Lincoln relics was held at the Library of Congress during the term of my appointment as Consultant in Poetry, 1974–1976. My only previous experience of living in Washington had been during World War II, when I was in military service (alluded to in Part 4). The apostrophe ("Mr. President . . .") at the close of Part 3 refers to the Watergate hearings and the subsequent resignation of President Nixon in 1974. In 1980, during the Carter administration, I was given the opportunity to read this poem at the White House.

Meditations on Death, "La Morte Meditata." My original version of Ungaretti's hermetic poem, titled "Death Thoughts," was written during his triumphal visit to the United States in the spring of 1970. By invitation of the Academy of American Poets, Ungaretti's American translators participated in his reading at the Guggenheim Museum in New York. Ungaretti (1888–1970) died shortly after his return to Italy.

NEXT-TO-LAST-THINGS

THE ABDUCTION. Elements of memory, dream, and fantasy en-
tered into the making of this poem, which was triggered by
my reading of *Missing Time*, a work on UFO abductions, by
Budd Hopkins (Richard Marek, 1981). See "The Layers:
Some Notes on 'The Abduction,'" in *Next-to-Last Things: New
Poems and Essays* (Atlantic Monthly Press, 1985).

THE SCENE. Alexander Blok (1880–1921), the most famous of
the Russian Symbolist poets, died in poverty and despair.

THE IMAGE-MAKER. In the teachings of Meister Eckhart (c.
1260–1327), German mystic and theologican, God is the only
true reality and the human soul is the only place in the universe
where God can reveal Himself in the truth of His being.

THREE SMALL PARABLES FOR MY POET FRIENDS. My in-
formation about the Bedouin beggar poets has its source in
The Manners and Customs of the Rwala Bedouins, by Alois
Musil (American Geographical Society, 1928).

THE WELLFLEET WHALE. Written in 1981 and first read at
Harvard that year as the Phi Beta Kappa poem. The actual
beaching of the whale, in Wellfleet Harbor, occurred on Sep-
tember 12, 1966.

NEW POEMS

MY MOTHER'S PEARS. For Carol and Greg Stockmal, of Worces-
ter, Massachusetts, whose annual gift of "my mother's pears"
inspired this poem.

CHARIOT. For Varujan Boghosian. Written for the retrospective exhibition of his work at the Hood Museum of Art, Dartmouth College, March 25–June 25, 1989. Boghosian's capacious studio, overflowing with materials for his constructions and collages, is located on the Dartmouth campus.

IN THE DARK HOUSE. The epigraph is from Primo Levi's last work *The Drowned and the Saved* (Summit Books, 1988). More than 42 years after his release from Auschwitz, Levi (1919–1987) jumped to his death in Turin, Italy, down the main stairwell of the apartment building in which he had been born.

   In the standard version of the myth of Orpheus and Eurydice, from which I depart in some details, as Orpheus approaches the exit from the underworld he succumbs to the temptation to look behind him to see if his bride is following. As a consequence of his impulsive behavior, Eurydice is dragged back into Hades, doomed to languish there forever. In the land of the living, grief-stricken Orpheus is eventually torn into pieces by the Maenads, female attendants of Dionysus. Flung into the Hebrus, his head and his lyre float downriver to the sea, the head still crying out the name of his beloved and the lyre, "Apollo's priceless gift," still playing.

HORNWORM: SUMMER REVERIE, HORNWORM: AUTUMN LAMENTATION. The familiar tomato hornworm, dreaded because of its voracious appetite, is the larval stage of the beautiful and speedy hawkmoth, or sphinx moth, so called from the caterpillar's habit, when disturbed, of elevating the front part of its body and drawing back its head. Some observers find this posture more suggestive of a threatening cobra than of the enigmatic Sphinx of ancient Egypt and Greece. Hornworms are frequently parasitized by braconids, little ichneumon flies that inject eggs beneath their skin. The emerging larvae feed internally on the soft caterpillar tissues until they are mature enough to bore their way to the surface and form cocoons. By this time, death is near for the defenseless host.

THE SEA, THAT HAS NO ENDING . . . Philip Guston (1913–1980) was one of the major American painters of his generation. My poem incorporates memories of him and of our conversations.

PROTEUS. "In the myth of Proteus we are told that at midday he rose from the flood and slept in the shadow of the rocks of the coast. Around him lay the monsters of the deep, whom he was charged with tending. He was famous for his gift of prophecy, but it was a painful art, which he was reluctant to employ. The only way anyone could compel him to foretell the future was by pouncing on him while he slept in the open. It was in order to escape the necessity of prophesying that he changed his shape . . . If he saw that his struggles were useless, he resumed his ordinary appearance, spoke the truth, and plunged back into the sea." —From "Poet of Transformations," in the collection of my essays, *A Kind of Order, A Kind of Folly* (Atlantic-Little, Brown, 1975); originally published in *The New Republic*, January 23, 1965.

TOUCH ME. The opening line is recalled from "As Flowers Are," in my *Selected Poems 1928–1958* (Atlantic-Little, Brown, 1958).

ACKNOWLEDGMENTS

My thanks to the publications in which these poems have previously appeared:

"My Mother's Pears," "Proteus," "Halley's Comet," "Touch Me":
  The New Yorker
"In the Dark House": *The Atlantic Monthly*
"Chariot": *The Gettysburg Review*. First published in *Varujan Bogh-
  osian: A Retrospective* (Hood Museum of Art, Dartmouth Col-
  lege, Hanover, New Hampshire, 1989). Reprinted in *The Best
  American Poetry 1992*, edited by Louise Glück.
"The Sea, That Has No Ending . . .": *Transforming Vision: Writers
  on Art*, selected and introduced by Edward Hirsch (The Art
  Institute of Chicago, 1994).
"My Mother's Pears," "Proteus," "The Sea That Has No End-
  ing . . .": *Poetry Ireland Review*, Special North American Issue.
"Hornworm: Summer Reverie," "Hornworm: Autumn Lamenta-
  tion": *The American Poetry Review*.

Publications in which some of the earlier poems in this collection
  first appeared include *The American Poetry Review, Antaeus,
  Art in America, The Atlantic Monthly, Book Week, Craft Hori-
  zons, Iowa Review, Malahat Review, The Nation, New Ameri-
  can Review, New England Review, The New Leader, The New
  Yorker, The New York Quarterly, The New York Review of
  Books, The New York Times, Partisan Review, Poetry, Salma-
  gundi, The Times Literary Supplement* (London).

INDEX